Discovering

FUNGI

Jennifer Coldrey

The Bookwright Press
New York · 1988

Discovering Nature

Discovering Ants
Discovering Bees and Wasps
Discovering Beetles
Discovering Birds of Prey
Discovering Butterflies and Moths
Discovering Crabs and Lobsters
Discovering Crickets and Grasshoppers
Discovering Damselflies and Dragonflies
Discovering Ducks and Geese
Discovering Flies

Discovering Flowering Plants
Discovering Freshwater Fish
Discovering Frogs and Toads
Discovering Fungi
Discovering Rabbits and Hares
Discovering Rats and Mice
Discovering Saltwater Fish
Discovering Sea Birds
Discovering Slugs and Snails
Discovering Snakes and Lizards
Discovering Spiders
Discovering Squirrels
Discovering Worms

Further titles are in preparation

All photographs from Oxford Scientific Films

First published in the
United States in 1988 by
The Bookwright Press
387 Park Avenue South
New York, NY 10016

First published in 1987 by
Wayland (Publishers) Limited
61 Western Road, Hove
East Sussex BN3 1JD, England

© Copyright 1987 Wayland (Publishers) Limited

ISBN 0–531–18170–7

Library of Congress Catalog Card Number: 87–71745

Typeset by DP Press Limited, Sevenoaks, Kent
Printed in Italy by Sagdos S.p.A., Milan

Cover *Cup fungi can be found growing on bare ground and in the woods.*

Frontispiece *Two creamy-capped toadstools grow from a stump in an English oak wood.*

Contents

1
Introducing Fungi

This fungus, growing on a dead branch, looks like a crinkled blob of slimy yellow jelly.

What are Fungi?

To many people, fungi are a strange and unfamiliar group of "plants." Mushrooms and toadstools are some of the best known examples, but there are hundreds of other kinds of fungi too. There are funnel or cup-shaped forms, rounded puffballs, slimy blobs or shelf-like outgrowths from trees, fluffy mildews on plant stems and leaves, and cobweb-like molds on rotten wood or stale food. There are many other fungi that we never see because they can only be seen with a microscope, or because they grow underground or inside other plants or animals.

Some of the smallest fungi are the yeasts, so tiny they can only be seen under a microscope. At the other extreme are giant puffballs, some of which can measure over 1.5 m (5 ft) across. One of the largest fungi ever found was a huge bracket fungus growing on a tree in the state of Washington, in 1946. It measured 142 cm (56 in) long, 94 cm (37 in) wide and weighed 136 kg (300 lb).

Well over 60,000 different kinds of fungi are known to exist. They grow all over the world, in all kinds of places, ranging from the icy polar regions to the hot steamy tropics. Most fungi live in the soil and on the dead and rotting remains of plants and animals. Others live as **parasites** inside living plants and animals. Some live underwater, and there are even a few that invade our homes.

Although fungi are plant-like in some ways, they are not true plants because they do not contain the green pigment **chlorophyll**. This means they cannot make their own food, using energy from sunlight, like most plants. But they are not animals either, because they cannot take in

The giant puffball is one of the biggest fungi in the world.

and digest food inside their bodies as animals can. Biologists now place fungi in a kingdom of their own, neither as plants nor as animals.

The Body of a Fungus

Although there are fungi of many different shapes and sizes, they all have the same basic structure. Their bodies are made up of a collection of microscopic, tube-like threads called **hyphae**. These hyphae spread and branch among each other to form a fine web of interweaving threads, which is called a **mycelium**. The mycelia of many fungi look like delicate white cobwebs.

We can see the body of a fungus only after the threads have formed a mycelium – each hypha is far too small to be seen with the naked eye. Scientists measure hyphae in **micrometers**, one micrometer being one thousandth of a millimeter (which is 0.04 in). Most fungal hyphae are between 10 and 50 micrometers

Growing on some old tea bags, the mycelium of this mold fungus forms a delicate white cobweb.

wide, but some can be as small as ½ micrometer, while others may be as large as 100 micrometers across. In many fungi the hyphae are divided into cells by cross walls; in others the hyphae form long, continuous tubes.

Unlike most land plants, the body of a fungus is not divided into roots, stems and leaves. However, in many fungi, groups of hyphae sometimes clump together to form a different kind of structure – the fruiting body. This may be quite large and is usually the only part of a fungus we can see and recognize. Mushrooms and toadstools are the fruiting bodies of fungi whose mycelia live underground or are hidden inside the wood of a rotting log or tree trunk.

Yeasts are somewhat different because they do not have hyphae. Their bodies consist of just one, tiny, egg-shaped cell about 5 micrometers long. Yeasts normally live together in

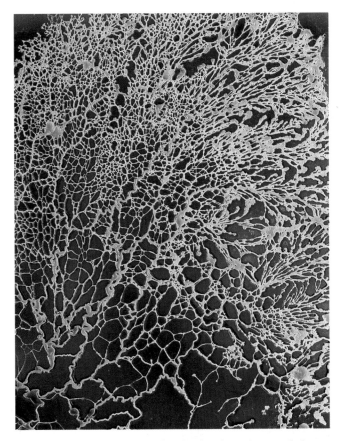

When highly magnified, the hyphae of this fungus can be seen branching and spreading to form a lace-like mycelium.

large numbers. They multiply rapidly to form big groups of cells.

2
How Fungi Live and Grow

This soft, fleshy fungus lives and grows by feeding on the wood of both dead and living trees.

Food and Feeding

Fungi take in their food by absorbing it through the thin walls of their hyphae. They need to live close to their food supply so that the hyphae can spread through it and absorb the nourishment from it. Hyphae absorb water and various useful minerals in this way. But fungi need other kinds of food too, including sugar, starch and protein. Unlike green plants, they cannot make these important foods themselves.

Most fungi obtain these vital foods by living on the dead remains of other living things. These fungi are called **saprophytes**. Their hyphae produce special chemicals that ooze out into the dead plant or animal **tissues**, breaking them down into simpler substances that the hyphae can then absorb. The fungus is really "digesting" food outside its body before absorbing it. Fungi that live among dead leaves, on rotting wood, or in dung or compost heaps, are all saprophytes. So are the molds that grow on stale bread, cheese or leather, since these are all materials produced from living things.

Saprophytic fungi (together with **bacteria**) perform a very important job in nature because they help to rot down and clear away the dead bodies of plants and animals. The fungi remove some nutrients, but many others seep back into the soil to be used again by growing plants. Meanwhile, the broken-down plant remains form **humus**, a substance that improves the texture of the soil and helps to make it rich and fertile.

Other fungi obtain their food from living plants or animals. Most of these fungi are parasites and cause harm to the plant or animal they feed on. Their hyphae spread among the living cells,

pouring out chemicals that break down the tissues and thus allow the fungus to absorb the food. Many parasitic fungi eventually kill their **hosts**, but others do less damage.

These toadstools are saprophytes. They are growing on a cow-pat and absorbing food from it.

A puffball pushes its way up through the desert sands in Iran.

These dainty toadstools are living off dead leaves in a South American jungle.

Where Fungi Live

Fungi can survive in all kinds of places, provided there is plenty of food and moisture and a reasonable temperature for growth. One or two live in extremely cold conditions. Others thrive in very hot places, including the soils around hot springs or on volcanoes. Some heat-loving fungi do well inside compost heaps where the temperature is hot enough to kill most other **organisms**.

Many fungi live in soil where there is plenty of food. Some form their fruiting bodies underground. Others push their fruiting bodies above the ground in various shapes and forms. We can find these kinds of fungi growing in fields and other grassy places and also in woods. Some woodland fungi live in close association with the tree roots underground; others grow as saprophytes on dead logs and tree stumps, or as parasites on living trees.

Underwater fungi are found in freshwater ponds and streams and a few live in the ocean. They are mostly microscopic, often transparent and very fragile. Many grow on floating and submerged leaves or on other decaying plants and animals. Others live on fish or as parasites on minute water plants called **algae**.

Fungi also live inside our homes, especially when the atmosphere is damp. We have probably all discovered bluish-green molds growing on old bread, fruit or jam, and noticed black sooty marks on the walls of a kitchen or bathroom. Fungi soon start to grow on damp walls and wood. The dry-rot fungus, often found in damp cellars and attics, feeds on lumber and destroys it as it grows. It spreads rapidly through wood and over damp brickwork and can eventually cause a house to collapse.

Sheets of white fungus grow over the wooden timbers of this damp, empty room.

Growing and Spreading

Provided a fungus has enough food, moisture, warmth and oxygen, it should grow well. Many grow in the dark without needing light. As the hyphae take in food, they lengthen, branching and spreading in all directions until a mycelium is formed. In many fungi, the mycelium grows out in a circle from a central point, provided there is nothing in its way. You can see this clearly when you find

Field mushrooms growing up through the grass in a "fairy ring."

a ring of toadstools in the grass. These are called "fairy rings." The toadstools are produced at the outer edges of the mycelium, which is growing underground. Fairy rings grow bigger every year as the mycelium keeps on spreading. Some are many feet in diameter and are estimated to be several hundred years old.

The mycelium of many fungi never becomes much more than a mass of tiny interwoven threads, which occasionally produce fruiting bodies. But in some fungi, bundles of hyphae cling together as they grow to form thicker strands, sometimes well over 1mm (0.04 in) thick. These tough, cord-like strands, which are called **rhizomorphs**, allow the fungus to spread more widely, even over places where there is no available food or water. The outer hyphae often have thick, protective walls, while the inner hyphae carry food and water to

These thick black rhizomorphs growing underneath the bark belong to the honey fungus, a deadly parasite of many trees.

support the fungus as it spreads.

Once a fungus has built up a good healthy mycelium, it will almost certainly produce fruiting bodies. These ripen, shed their **spores** and die, but the mycelium lives on. It will continue growing and spreading from year to year even though the older parts may die.

3
Reproduction

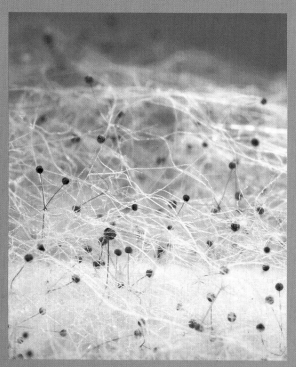

The round black sporangia of the common bread mold stick up like pinheads from the mycelium.

Producing Spores

Fungi multiply or **reproduce** themselves by forming spores. These develop on or inside some kind of fruiting body and in larger fungi they are produced by the million. Spores are microscopic in size; in fact, we can only see them when large numbers are puffed into the air like a cloud of dust. Different fungi produce spores of different shapes and sizes; some have thick walls, some thin; some are smooth while others have knobs or spikes on the surface; and some are white while others are colored pink, purple, black or brown.

Spores are rather like seeds because each one is capable of growing into a new fungus if it lands in a suitable place. However, unlike seeds, spores have no **embryo** plant or large stores of food inside them. They simply consist of just one or two cells with perhaps a drop of oil for food.

The simplest kinds of fungi (including many molds) produce spores in little round capsules at the ends of upright, unbranched hyphae. These capsules, called **sporangia**, stick up like pinheads from the mycelium – such fungi are often called pin molds. When ripe, the sporangium wall breaks down and the tiny spores drift away in the air. Many underwater fungi produce sporangia, but their spores are often specially adapted for floating or moving in water. Some have tail-like threads, which wiggle back and forth and allow the spores to swim.

Yeasts multiply by "budding." A small bud grows out from the parent and eventually cuts itself off to become a new individual. At certain times in their lives, however, yeasts also form spores, in groups of four, inside their cells.

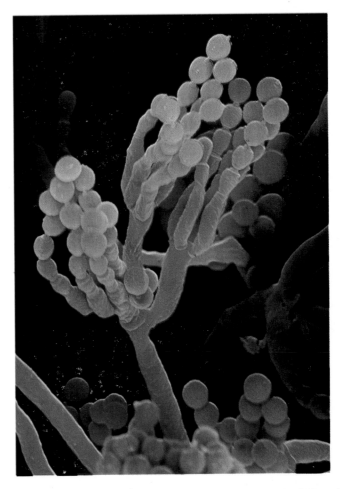

This photograph, taken under a powerful microscope, shows the spores of a penicillin mold; they are produced in open chains at the ends of short hyphae.

This section through a young field mushroom shows the developing pink gills and the ring of skin around the stalk.

These "velvet-foot" toadstools have small gills alternating with bigger ones.

Cap Fungi with Gills

The cap fungi, otherwise known as mushrooms and toadstools, produce their spores in umbrella-shaped fruiting bodies. These are larger and much more complicated than simple sporangia. They start to form when certain hyphae of the mycelium bunch together. These hyphae swell into button-like knobs, which eventually push their way out from under the soil or from inside a tree. They finally lengthen and expand to form the familiar toadstool shape.

Some young toadstools grow inside a kind of skin; when the stalk lengthens, this skin is broken, leaving a loose sheath at the base of the stalk and remnants of skin on top of the cap. Many young toadstools also have a kind of skin or veil across the underside of the cap. This gets broken as the cap expands, leaving a frill around the stalk and a ragged fringe around the edges of the cap.

Both the cap and stalk of a toadstool are made up of hyphae packed together in various ways. The cap is rather like a thick cushion on top, but underneath hang thin folds or "curtains" of tissue called **gills**. The gills radiate out from the stalk to the edge of the cap.

The spores are produced on the surface of the gills. The stalk of the toadstool holds the cap in a horizontal position well above the ground. When the spores are ripe, they drop down between the gills and are then carried away in currents of air.

There are hundreds of different cap fungi of various colors, shapes and sizes. Some are small and delicate with long, thin stems; others are more sturdy, with stout stalks. The cap may be flattish on top, or it may be steeply domed or bell-shaped. Some caps are dry and warty, some smooth and waxy-looking, while others are quite wet and slimy.

A mass of dainty "parasols" grows out from a dead tree stump.

Other Kinds of Cap Fungi

Not all cap fungi have gills. Instead, some produce their spores from the surface of small spines or teeth, which protrude from the underside of the cap. People sometimes call these hedgehog or tooth fungi.

Other fungi, including the *boletus* toadstools, have a cap whose underside looks rather like a sponge. It is peppered with holes or pores out of which the spores eventually fall. The large bracket fungi that grow on trees also have pores or tubes on the undersides of their caps. Their fruiting bodies are usually fan-shaped or semi-circular, and stick out from the tree like shelves. Some have a short stalk at one side, while others have no stalk at all.

Some bracket fungi grow to enormous size, up to half a meter (1 ½ ft) or more across. Their caps are often tough and leathery and some are almost like wood. Unlike most toadstools, which shed their spores and then shrivel and die after only a few days, many brackets last for several months. Some even live for several years, forming a new layer of

You can clearly see the holes beneath the cap of this sturdy boletus *toadstool.*

spore-producing tubes each year. These tubes, although very narrow, are absolutely vertical, so the spores do not hit the sides as they fall out. Many bracket fungi shed their spores only during wet weather. However, there is one large fungus, the common ganoderm, that sheds its spores continuously, both day and night, for

These large bracket fungi are growing in a tropical forest in Venezuela.

5 to 6 months of the year.

Whether a cap fungus has gills, spines or pores beneath its cap, the purpose is the same – to make a large surface from which huge numbers of spores can be produced.

Puffballs, Stinkhorns and Other Oddities

There are many fungi, related to cap fungi because of the type of spores they produce, that have very different kinds of fruiting bodies. Some form their spores on the outer surface of club-shaped or branched, coral-like outgrowths. Others have soft, jelly-like bodies that may be folded or wrinkled into a variety of unusual shapes. Some produce their spores inside ball-like "bags." These are the puffballs, a common group of fungi found in grassland and woodland where some grow on logs or tree stumps.

The fruiting body of a puffball is a rounded, thin-walled structure often on a short stalk. When ripe, it becomes full of dry, powdery spores. A hole usually forms at the top and spores are forced out of here in great puffs or clouds whenever a heavy drop of rain lands on the puffball. Other puffballs release their spores rather differently; they have no stalks and are not attached very firmly to the ground. When ripe, they break loose

Puffballs releasing clouds of dry, powdery spores into the air.

The tough outer skins of these tropical earthballs are splitting open to reveal the mass of black spores inside.

The lacy stinkhorn has a beautiful net-like veil around its stalk.

and, being so light, are easily blown along by the wind. The outer skin tears open and the spores spill out as the puffball tumbles along over the ground.

The earthballs and earthstar fungi (similar to puffballs) have thick, scaly, outer skins. This skin cracks and splits open when ripe, exposing the mass of spores to the wind.

The stinkhorns are curious and rather revolting fungi. They are common in woodlands where they grow up from beneath the soil or leaf mold. First a white, jelly-like, egg-shaped structure appears; then, out of this emerges a tall, tapering stem with a cone-shaped cap. The cap has a honeycomb pattern on its surface and is covered with an olive-green slime, containing the spores. The fungus gives off a disgusting smell and this attracts flies, which come to feed on the slimy spore mass.

Cup Fungi and Their Relatives

Some fungi produce their spores inside tiny bodies called **asci**. These form at the tips of certain hyphae. There are usually eight spores lined up in a row inside each ascus. When ripe, the asci swell with water. Their tips burst open and the spores are squirted out in a jelly-like liquid.

Many microscopic fungi, including some mildews and molds, produce spores from asci. So do some of the larger fungi, of which the cup fungi are some of the best known examples.

Above *The morel fungus produces its spores from inside the many pits and hollows of its crinkled head.*

Right *Cup fungi like this can be found in woodlands all over the world.*

Here the asci are grouped together to form a fruiting layer inside a shallow, cup-shaped fruiting body. The tips of the asci all point upward, toward the light; so, when the spores are ripe, they are fired up and out of the cup, sometimes for several inches into the air, and get carried away by the wind.

Cup fungi can be found growing on bare ground and in woodland where some grow on trees. They range from a few mm to several inches across.

Other fungi have the fruiting layer of asci arranged in a more complicated way on the fruiting body. The candle-snuff fungus has asci hidden inside tiny cavities on its branching stems. The larger morels, with their sturdy stalks, produce their asci as a lining to the many pits and hollows on their crinkled, cone-shaped heads.

Even more unusual are the underground truffles. These are round, warty lumps whose asci line a maze of tubes inside the fungus. Their spores

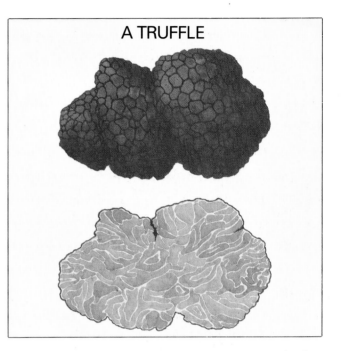

A TRUFFLE

The lower drawing is a section through the truffle, showing the maze of spore-filled chambers.

are never released; but they can get carried away if the truffle is dug up or eaten by an animal such as a mouse, squirrel or deer. Spores that are eaten come out in the animal's droppings and grow in a new patch of ground.

The Dispersal and Growth of Spores

Fungal spores are so light and tiny that they are easily carried away by the wind or in currents of air. The atmosphere is full of them as they constantly rain down onto the ground, both outside and inside our homes. A common mushroom, for example, produces half a million spores a minute.

If all these spores grew into fungi we would be buried beneath them. Fortunately out of the many millions of spores that are produced, only a few land on a suitable place for growth. Besides needing food, water, oxygen and warmth, a spore needs space in which to grow. Many spores are prevented from growing because of competition from other fungi. If conditions are right, the spore starts to swell and to push out one or two

This bracket fungus can shed twenty million spores a minute. You can see the brown spores covering the tree trunk.

small hyphal tubes. These grow and put out branches as they spread. So a new fungus is born.

Most fungi have some way of shooting or dropping their spores into the air. This increases their chances of being spread far and wide. In many cases, part of the fruiting body swells with moisture and then explodes; the spores are either shot off in a stream of liquid or they are pushed off by a drop of water.

Not all fungi depend on the wind to spread their spores. Some fungi produce slimy spores, which glide away in rain or moisture, while many **aquatic** fungi have spores that can swim or float. Insects also help to spread fungal spores – the stinkhorns rely on flies to carry their spores away, and there are many wood-eating beetles and other insects that carry spores on their bodies as they fly from tree to tree.

Flies spread the spores of the stinkhorn fungus as they feed on the slime and carry spores away with them on their bodies.

4
Fungi and Other Living Things

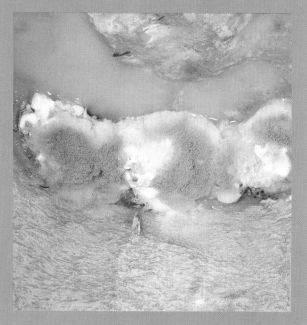

This overripe pumpkin is slowly rotting as molds grow over its soft, juicy flesh.

Fungi as Plant Pests

Many plants become damaged, diseased or even killed by parasitic fungi that live and feed on them. Farmers and gardeners are especially aware of this because numerous fungi attack our flowers and crops. Mildews grow on the leaves of hops, vines, roses and various trees. The familiar powdery white coat consists of the mycelium and spores of the fungus.

"Rusts" are another group of microscopic fungi thay infect many cereals, grasses and numerous wild plants. They live inside the leaves, their spores bursting out at the surface to form reddish-brown, rusty-looking patches. Once the leaves of a plant are damaged, they lose water and cannot continue to make food, so the plant eventually wilts and dies.

"Smuts" attack the flowers of grasses and cereals. They are so named because of the sooty mass of spores they produce. Grasses and cereals such as barley and rye are also seriously affected by a disease known as "ergot." The fungus produces small, dark, banana-shaped bodies that grow in place of the flowers, thus destroying the developing seeds or grains.

Apples, pears, tomatoes and many other fruits become rotten and moldy as a result of fungi growing on them. Potatoes often suffer from potato blight, a serious fungal disease. Potato blight totally destroyed the potato crop in Ireland during the 1840's, leading to widespread famine in the country.

Many soil-living fungi attack the roots of plants; others kill seeds and young seedlings in the ground.

Fungi can also kill trees. Some grow up through the wood, or just beneath the bark, from underground. Others

Here a smut fungus has infected the flowering shoots of barley.

land, as spores, on small cracks or wounds on trunks and branches and from here their hyphae grow into the tree.

Fungi as Animal Pests

Animals suffer from fungal infections too. Moles, rabbits and mice sometimes inhale the spores of soil-living fungi when they breathe. The fungi start to grow inside their lungs, causing lung diseases that usually end in the death of the animal. Birds and also humans often suffer from similar lung infections. These fungi, which behave as animal parasites inside the lungs, are often fungi that normally live as saprophytes feeding on dead remains in the soil or on rotting vegetation.

Several fungi live on the skin, fur or feathers of animals. These parasites do not usually kill their hosts, but they often cause pain or discomfort. Humans commonly suffer from fungal infections of the skin; "ringworm," often found on the scalp, is caused, not by a worm, but by a fungus that attacks and destroys the hair. "Athlete's foot" occurs on the skin between the toes; here the fungus first starts to grow by living on dead layers of skin, but it later attacks the living layers beneath, and this can be painful and irritating.

Fish are often infected by fungi.

This tiger beetle is being killed by a fungus infection. You can see the fluffy white mold growing out from its joints.

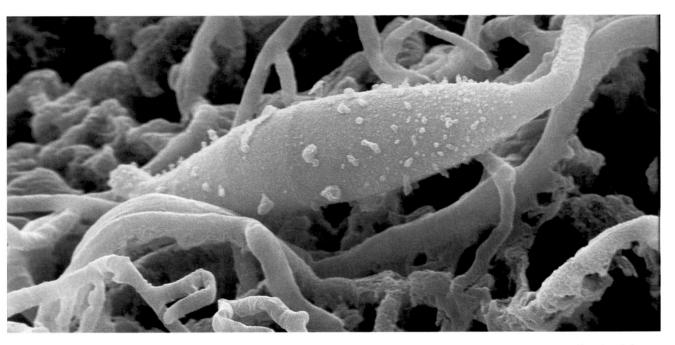

The fungus causing "ringworm" looks like this when it is magnified 1,800 times under an electron microscope.

They appear on the fins and scales as moldy white blotches but many penetrate inside the body, eventually killing the fish. Insects and their **larvae** are also killed by parasitic fungi, which grow inside their bodies.

Many fungi contain poisons that can kill or harm both humans and other animals if they are eaten. Several toadstools are known to be deadly to humans. The ergots of cereals also contain lethal poisons that cause severe illness or death; cattle sometimes die from grazing on hay or grasses that are infected with ergot.

Plant Partnerships

Some fungi live in a close relationship with plants yet do not kill or harm them. One example can be seen in woodland soils where the mycelia of many toadstools live closely attached to the roots of certain trees. These associations are called **mycorrhizae**.

Fly agaric toadstools often grow in pine woods where they form mycorrhizae with the roots of the trees.

The fungal hyphae cover the smaller tree roots like a mantle; some even grow inside the roots to form a fine network in the outer layers. The tree roots become shorter, fatter and more branched than normal, but do not die.

Both partners seem to benefit from the relationship. The fungus absorbs vital sugars from the tree, while in return it takes in important minerals from the soil and passes them on to the tree. In poor soils especially, the fungi seem to help the tree roots to absorb food more easily and therefore the trees grow better than they would otherwise.

Some fungi live in an even closer relationship with plants. They have microscopic plants called algae growing among their hyphae. This combination of a fungus with an alga is called a **lichen**.

Lichens often grow on bare, exposed places such as walls, rocks or

Several different lichens are growing on these rocks, just above high tide level on the seashore.

tree trunks. Many form flat, encrusting plates of tissue; others are more leaf-like or like tiny shrubs, while a few hang in long tassels from the trees. The fungus gives the main shape to the lichen and it also forms fruiting bodies on the surface. However, it could not survive without the algae from which it absorbs sugars and vitamins. The algae, meanwhile, are protected from drying out and from the cold; they also obtain some water and minerals from the fungus. Each partner helps the other to survive, often in places where neither could live alone.

This cross section of a lichen shows the fungal hyphae wrapped around the tiny algal cells.

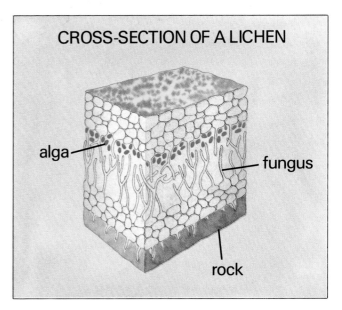

CROSS-SECTION OF A LICHEN

alga

fungus

rock

Animal Partnerships

Some ants and certain other insects have an unusual association with fungi, which has advantages for both partners.

Many wood-boring beetles carry spores or bits of fungus on their bodies when they fly from one tree to another. As they feed on the young leaves or tunnel into the wood, they introduce the fungus into the tree where it soon grows and spreads. Ambrosia beetles carry a fungus into the **sapwood** of trees they visit. The fungus feeds and grows on the wood and soon a creamy-white mold lines the walls of the beetles' tunnels. The beetles feed on the fungus, and the spores form the chief food for their grubs when they hatch.

Some ants positively encourage the growth of certain fungi inside their nests. Many ants build the walls of

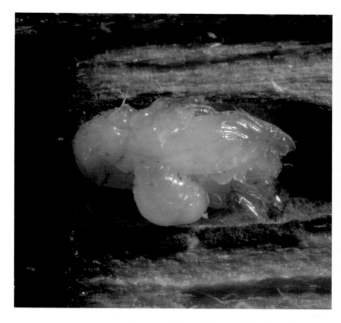

Two young ambrosia beetles. The larger creature in this picture is a pupa, from which an adult beetle will emerge.

their nests from chewed-up wood and other plant matter. Some allow a particular type of fungus to live in the walls; it seems to strengthen and bind the walls together as it grows. Only this one fungus is allowed to grow inside the nest; the ants vigorously remove all other fungi to prevent their eggs and young from becoming moldy or rotten.

The South American leaf-cutter ants cultivate a special fungus inside their nests in order to feed themselves and their young. These ants crop and take home the leaves from jungle trees. They cut them up and chew them into fine pieces, then they plant the leaves in special chambers where they introduce the fungus and allow it to grow. The fungus feeds and thrives on the chewed-up leaves, producing clusters of sweet, round swellings, which the ants and their larvae eat. The ants constantly tend their "fungus garden," removing all other fungi that start to grow.

Leaf-cutter ants from Trinidad busily at work in their "fungus garden."

Enemies and Survival

Larger fungi, in particular, provide food for many animals. Toadstools are nibbled by mice, voles, rabbits and squirrels. Slugs and snails eat them too, while larger animals, including deer, pigs and domestic cattle, also enjoy them. Even carnivores, like wolves and bear, eat fungi occasionally, and so do we humans.

Insects, too, can damage fungi; many flies and beetles lay their eggs inside them, and the grubs feed on the fungus when they hatch. Some insects also eat the spores of fungi.

In all these cases, it is mainly the fruiting bodies of fungi that are eaten and destroyed. The mycelium goes on growing, either underground or inside a tree, so the fungus itself is not

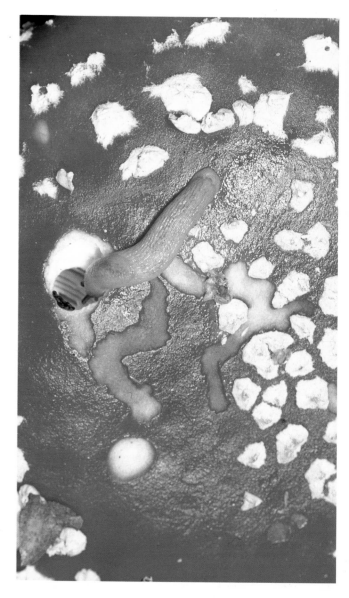

A slug settles down to a meal on the cap of a fly agaric toadstool.

actually killed. Some trees and other plants produce poisons in their bark, leaves or roots that can prevent fungi from growing on them. But, in general, fungi seem to have very few enemies that can completely destroy them. Their main rivals are other fungi or bacteria, which can compete with them for food and space. Many fungi overcome these enemies by producing poisonous substances called **antibiotics**, which kill other fungi and bacteria.

Most fungi cannot survive in extremely hot or cold conditions, when the delicate mycelium will shrivel or die. However, some manage to survive by forming special thick-walled "resting" spores; others produce hard, roundish balls of tightly packed hyphae called **sclerotia**. When better conditions return, these resting stages will grow and produce spores, which develop into new young fungi.

One type of fungus may kill another. Here a parasitic mold feeds on a toadstool.

Fungi and Humans

Fungi affect the lives of humans in many ways. They cause disease, both to ourselves and our domestic animals. They also cause serious damage to many of our crops and they are a nuisance when they grow inside our houses, either on our food or on wood and other fabrics. Fortunately, we can control most of these fungal "pests" by treating them with **fungicides**, chemical sprays or powders that kill them.

But despite the problems they cause, fungi are also extremely valuable to humans. They are useful as food; the cultivated mushroom is now grown and eaten on an enormous scale in many parts of the world, and people enjoy eating many other kinds of fungi too. Fungi also provide important vitamins and flavors, which are used in many foods.

Yeasts play a vital part in the brewing industry and in the making of wine, cider and other alcoholic drinks. When they are put into a sugary solution, such as grape juice or malted barley, yeasts grow and multiply rapidly. They feed on the

Common mushrooms are grown commercially in huge underground cellars in northern France.

sugars, changing or "fermenting" them into alcohol and a gas called carbon dioxide. The gas causes the fizziness in many alcoholic drinks. The same fermentation process is used in bread-making; here the yeasts react with sugars in the dough. They produce bubbles of gas, which causes the dough to rise. Yeasts contain lots of protein; they are used commercially to make valuable foodstuffs for both

Yeasts are an essential part of the bread-making process.

humans and animals.

Some of our most useful medicines come from fungi. The most famous are the antibiotics, substances that can kill bacteria and other germs. Penicillin, produced by a blue mold, was the first antibiotic to be discovered, in 1929.

5
Learning More About Fungi

These beautiful and brightly colored waxy-cap toadstools can often be found under pine trees.

Look for fungi wherever you go, both indoors and outside. You are almost certain to find some growing in all but the driest weather. However, in the northern United States and parts of Canada, autumn is the best time to go out and search for wild fungi. At that time of year the weather is damp and not too cold, and many larger fungi will be putting up their fruiting bodies.

Notice which fungi grow in the grass, or which prefer to live on trees. Look among rotting leaves and twigs on the woodland floor, on dead tree stumps and on old logs. Keep a notebook to record your finds and always note the date, the place you found your fungi and what the weather was like. Make drawings or take photographs of the fungi you see – you will then be able to look them up in a book to find out more about them. Notice the shapes, colors, smells and textures of different fungi, but never taste them – they may be poisonous. Try to discover how they produce their spores and whether a toadstool has gills or pores under its cap.

You can find out more about the spores of cap fungi by making spore prints on paper. Try with a ripe mushroom first. Cut off the stalk about 5 mm (0.2 in) beneath the cap (picture 1). Place the cap, gills downward, on a sheet of white paper. Cover it with a large bowl to prevent drafts and leave it for an hour or two (2). Then, carefully pick the cap off the paper. You should find a spore pattern that exactly matches the arrangement of the gills. If you want to keep the print, spray fixative above it (3).

You can try making a spore print with toadstools to compare the color and arrangement of the gills. Use dark paper if you think the spores may be white or pale in color. If you want to look at spores or fungal hyphae in more detail you will have to use a microscope.

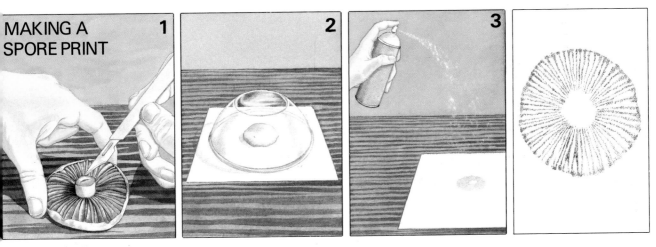

MAKING A SPORE PRINT

1 2 3

Glossary

Algae (singular alga): simple, non-flowering plants, most of which live in water. Many are microscopic in size.

Antibiotics: substances, produced by some molds and other fungi, that can kill or harm other microscopic fungi and bacteria.

Aquatic: living in water.

Asci (singular ascus): tiny, spore-containing structures produced by some types of fungi.

Bacteria: microscopic organisms found in abundance in almost every kind of habitat. Many cause diseases in animals and plants.

Chlorophyll: the green coloring in plants that enables them to absorb energy from sunlight and change simple chemicals into sugars and other food.

Embryo (plant): the young plant inside the seed.

Fungicides: poisonous chemicals used by humans (either in spray or powder form) to kill fungal pests.

Gills: thin folds of tissue, hanging beneath the caps of many cup fungi, on which spores are produced.

Host: an animal or plant on which a parasite lives.

Humus: the soft, moist, dark brown material in soil, made from decaying plant and animal remains.

Hyphae (singular hypha): microscopic, branching, thread-like filaments from which all fungi, except yeasts, are made.

Larvae (singular larva): the young grub-like stage of most insects (also young stage of certain other animals) that hatches from the egg.

Lichen: plant-like organism made up from the combination of a fungus and an alga.

Micrometer: one thousandth of a millimeter (1 mm equals 0.04 in).

Mycelium: the mass of interwoven hyphae that makes up the main body of a fungus.

Mycorrhizae: the close association between a fungus and the roots of a plant, in which both partners benefit.

Organism: any living creature.

Parasite: an animal or plant that lives in or on the body of another.

Reproduce: to multiply and produce new individuals of the same kind.

Rhizomorphs: tough strands of fungal tissue made up of many closely packed hyphae, which often spread over long distances.

Saprophyte: a plant (or plant-like organism) that feeds on the dead remains of animals and plants.

Sapwood: the soft, outer layers of young and recently formed wood beneath the bark of a tree.

Sclerotia (singular sclerotium): tough, roundish or cigar-shaped bodies, composed of a mass of tightly packed hyphae, which can survive in very cold, hot or dry conditions.

Sporangia (singular sporangium): round, stalked capsules, containing spores, formed by many smaller fungi.

Spore: the single-celled unit from which a new fungus can grow.

Tissue: a mass of cells of one particular type, which forms a specialized part of a plant or animal body. Skin, muscle or wood are all types of tissue.

Finding Out More

The following books will tell you more about fungi.

An Index of the Common Fungi of North America by O.K. Miller, Jr., and D.F. Farr. Lubrecht and Kramer, 1985.

Mushrooms by Sylvia A. Johnson. Lerner Publications, 1986.

Mushrooms and Other Fungi by Aurel Dermek. Arco, 1985.

Mushrooms and Molds by Robert Froman. Crowell Junior Books, 1972.

Mushrooms and Toadstools: A Colour Field Guide by U. Nonis. Hippocrene Books, 1983.

The New Field Guide to Fungi by Eric Soothill and Alan Farrhurst. Transatlantic, 1979.

Index

The numbers in **bold** refer to the pictures.

Picture Acknowledgments

All photographs from Oxford Scientific Films by the following photographers: G.I. Bernard 8, 12, 14 (bottom), 15, 20 (top), 21, 23, 26 (left), 30, 31, 35, 36, 40; M. Canis 33, David Cayless 26 (right); Waina Cheng 25 (bottom); J.A.L. Cooke 10, 14 (top), 18, 37; Michael Fogden 25 (top), 42, *cover*; Philip Goddard 13; Manfred Kage 19; G.A. Maclean 20 (bottom), Richard Packwood *frontispiece*, 24, 34; Robin Redfern 16; P.K. Sharpe 32; Tim Shepherd 17, 22; Perry D. Slocum (Earth Scenes) 39; David Vinter 9; Barrie E. Watts 11, 28, 29, 38; The photograph on p.41 is from the Bread Information Bureau; The illustrations are by David Webb.